Unconditional
LOVE AND FAITH
OBSERVED

BILL BELKNAP

WestBow Press books may be ordered through booksellers or by contacting:

WestBow Press
A Division of Thomas Nelson & Zondervan
1663 Liberty Drive
Bloomington, IN 47403
www.westbowpress.com
1 (866) 928-1240

ISBN: 978-1-4908-8495-0 (sc)
ISBN: 978-1-4908-8494-3 (e)

Library of Congress Control Number: 2015909731

Print information available on the last page.

WestBow Press rev. date: 09/11/2015

REFERENCES

Common Prayer by Shane Claiborne, Jonathan Wilson-Hartgrove, and Enuma Okoro, Publisher - Zondervan (The only reference to this book is for its use in prayer meetings, there are no quotations)

Heaven by Randy Alcorn, Publisher - Tyndale House Publishers, Inc.

Revival by Adam Hamilton, Publisher - Abingdon Press

A Grief Observed by C. S. Lewis, Publisher - Zondervan

Making Sense of the Bible by Adam Hamilton, Publisher - Harper One

The One Year Bible, Publisher - Crossway (The only reference to this book is for its use in daily study, there are no quotes from the ESV Bible)

Keeping Hope Alive by Lewis Smedes, Publisher - Thomas Nelson

DEDICATION

To my wife Donna Kaye and my son Bill.
To Donna, because this essay would never have
been written without her love and Faith teachings.
To Bill, for his love, professional help and
encouragement to publish.

CONTENTS

PREFACE

Soon after my wife Donna Kaye's death, I acknowledged her love and Faith in God, me and all people with the epitaph on her tomb stone "True Love Knows No Bounds". And shortly after that, I wrote a long poem regarding her life using 'True Love Knows No Bounds" as its theme. The writing of this poem gave me the idea of writing an essay about learning the true meaning of unconditional love and Faith from Donna. A good friend had given me C. S, Lewis's book "A Grief Observed" which also prompted me to consider more seriously writing about Donna. After much deliberation and prayer, and with God's divine help, I began my writing.

Since my background was engineering and executive management, writing about love and Faith was new to me, but with God's help, the more I wrote the easier my writing became.

In this essay, I have openly and truthfully described my experiences in everyday life of learning the importance of love and Faith in our everyday living. Our unconditional Faith in God, and the importance of frequent prayer in asking for and allowing God to lead us throughout our lives are emphasized by recounting my personal life experiences.

Not only have I memorialize Donna's part in teaching me about love and Faith, but at the encouragement of my son, I have written about the significant experiences throughout my entire life regarding love and Faith, and how God has always been there helping me. We constantly have God's help directing us through our lives without really knowing or acknowledging that He is there taking care of us.

Acknowledgements

First and foremost, God must be acknowledged for His part in my writing this essay. It would never have been written if God had not encouraged me to write and told me that He would help me. And, He has always been there helping me, as I have acknowledged throughout my essay. God is always doing wonderful things for us, we need only to relax and listen to Him.

My mom and dad, my first wife, Carolyn, and our children, Barbara Ann and Bill C. all provided me with unconditional love and Faith during my early life. When we are young we do not think much about these emotions and Beliefs, but in retrospect they were always there and are very important to our lives. My immediate family gave me the roots for a lifetime of unconditional love and Faith in God and in them. My essay relates a few of our family experiences of God taking good care of us and helping us to do what was best for us in our times of need.

My son, Bill C. has been of immeasurable help to me, not only by caring for and comforting me in my grief, but in writing this essay. His review of my writing and encouragement have prompted and helped me make the decision to have my essay published. He not only gave me good professional advise about content, he encouraged me to write about my earlier life, and gave me good advise about spelling, grammar and organization. My son has owned and operated a very successful sound recording studio for over 30 years. He professionally writes and performs music and lyrics and overlays sound to video commercials and films. However, the greatest and most heart warming experience for me, from my son reviewing my essay, was learning that he believes in God and Jesus Christ much the same as I do. And also, from his encouraging me to publish my essay in order that it might help others in their understanding of Faith and in their relationship with God. His early Christian education at home and in church and Sunday school were successful.

Tari Carbaugh, associate pastor at Bartlesville First Church, has been of tremendous help to me throughout my grief journey and in writing this essay. She is a very upbeat and happy person, always looking at the bright side of life. Tari and I enjoyed several serious discussions about Beliefs, Faith, and Biblical references before and during the early writing of my essay. She encouraged me to write about God's Perfection in His Faith and love for each of us. She reviewed my essay during the early writing, and encouraged me to show it to my son regarding content and publication. At Tari's suggestion and with my help we organized a small men's prayer group consisting of seven older men recently widowed from losing their wives. We have been meeting for about four months at a local McDonalds at 9:30 on Wednesday mornings. For these prayer meetings we use a book "Common Prayer" by Claiborne, Wilson-Hartgrove and Okoro. Tari does a fantastic job of leading our devotional with her Christ like, cherrie, sunshine personality. Starting our prayer meetings we measure each of our spirit feelings on a scale of one to ten, and during our meetings we pray for all of those persons we know that need prayer. The McDonalds' personnel like our coming there and using their facility, in fact they occasionally ask for prayers. These prayer meetings and the camaraderie developed among seven old men with a common spiritual need is phenomenal. It has been so great that Tari has started a similar prayer group for young adult singles which is also proving to be very successful.

My wife, Donna Kaye, must be acknowledged, for without her this essay would never have been written. Donna Kaye's unconditional love and Faith in God first and foremost, then in me and in the world prompted me to study and in turn write about unconditional love and Faith. My poem, her epitaph, our church sign, and my prayer all needed to be brought together to memorialize Donna's wonderful beliefs and attitude toward life and people. I know that she would encourage publication of my essay because it might help others to Believe and accept God and Jesus Christ. In Randy Alcorn's book "Heaven" he eloquently describes Donna's and my emotional feelings for God and for each other: "Though it is possible to put people over God (which is idolatry), it is possible, while putting God over people, to find in people a wonderful expression of God himself, so great that it is completely appropriate for us to have them in our hearts, to find joy in them, and long to be with them. Such sentiments are not idolatry, and it is not wrong to have them. In fact, something is wrong if we do not have them. For finding joy in God and longing for God does not kill our joy in longing for others. Rather it fuels it. The joy and longing we have for other people is directly derived from our joy in and longing for God." Alcorn's words in this quote very accurately describe my feelings toward God and Donna Kaye. And, they accurately describe Donna's frequently expressed feelings toward God, me and people. My analysis of Alcorn's statement, is that it really puts into perspective our emotional need to always put God first in everything and never let someone or something become an idol above or before God, we should always remember that our love for another person can actually reenforce our love for God and Jesus Christ.

The authors of the books referenced in my essay need to be recognized because of the great help their books have been to me in studying Donna's philosophy and my life, and in my understanding of God's role in all of our lives. They are named in my essay as I have quoted from their works or referenced their ideas. In addition to those in my essay, in Adam Hamilton's book "Revival", he documents John Wesley's life as "Faith as Wesley lived it". John Wesley founded the Methodist church in England and lived a life completely surrendered to God. Following is quoted Wesley's prayer of surrender to God which expresses my Beliefs well:

I am no longer my own, but thine.
Put me to what though wilt, rank me with whom thou wilt.
Put me to doing, put me to suffering.
Let me be employed for thee or laid aside for thee,
exalted for thee or brought low for thee.

Let me be full, let me be empty.
Let me have all things, let me have nothing.
I freely and heartily yield all things
to thy pleasure and disposal.
And now, O glorious and blessed God,
Father, Son, and Holy Spirit,
thou art mine, and I am thine. So be it.
And the covenant which I have made on earth,
let it be ratified in Heaven. Amen.

Wow, what a prayer, if we could only Believe in God and live our lives as John Wesley did and so beautifully expressed in this prayer.

Many dear friends have also helped me with my essay. Some of them, without knowing they were helping, but by showing their sincere and true Belief in God and Jesus Christ in many different ways, and by showing their love for me, they have been very helpful to me. Some of these helpful, good and faithful friends include the following: Tari Carbaugh, Kevin Tully, Stu and Linda Fenton, Donna Kaye King, Jene and Nancy Dewey, Luke and Cheryl Cowles, Judy and Dave Scroggins, Amanda Allen, Dixie Squires, Mariana Guerrero, Carolyn Brinkmeyer, Millie and Don Ryan, John Thompson, Cecilia Page, Colleen Oldfather, Dixie Allen, Felix Braggs, Helen Bumpus, and Joy and Chuck Tennell. Joy Tennell is a very special blessing to me because we often discuss the Bible. And, from her good knowledge of the Bible, she has been and is continually very helpful in teaching me and helping me understand God's word. It is very special and wonderful to have so many good, loyal friends to comfort you and to continually show their love for you in good times as well as in times of sorrow and need.

What are Unconditional Love and Faith

It has taken me nearly all of my life to really began to think about and understand what unconditional Love and Faith are all about and to begin to appreciate the deep meaning of these terms. They are terms, not just mere words, for the meaning of "terms" is words with very precise and limited meanings, and this is certainly true regarding Love and Faith.

When do we begin to relate to what we have observed and learned about Love and Faith? It must be in our very early beginning of life when crying as a baby for our mother to show her love by picking us up and hugging us, or when we are crying for milk or for her to change our diaper. Nearly every mother has unconditional love for her baby and the babies have unconditional love for and faith in their mothers. It is almost universally instinctive for this relationship to occur. This show of love and faith from a baby for mother and from a mother for her baby must be truly the purest and most basic expression of unconditional love and faith. A mother will normally give her baby whatever her baby needs and wants without any reservations and the baby will accept whatever is given. The same is true for nearly all animal life. This is one of God's greatest blessings and gifts to us when He created life in the universe.

I know my mother loved me unconditionally, she was always there when I needed or wanted her. She taught me about Jesus Christ, sin and the ten commandments as a small child. My mom and dad were very strict regarding my activities up through high school. Boy Scouts, church and band were my main activities outside of school, some sports, but sports were not emphasized then like they are today. Mom was a school teacher and expected top grades. I recall there was one girl I thought I liked when I was a junior in high school. She and her family belonged to another religious faith. My mother talked to me about the differences in religious beliefs and suggested that I find someone else to date. She was taking care of and looking after me with love and faith and I respected her judgement by dating other girls.

During college I dated several girls my first two years, and then fell in love with my wife to be, Carolyn Crandell, during our junior year. It was a sincere romance with both of us knowing in our hearts that we were meant for each other, it was unconditional love and faith, a blessing from God. The following summer I worked on laying an oil company pipeline and then spent all of my earnings on an engagement ring for Carolyn. We were married the week before college graduation the next year. Although I was not looking for messages from God at that time in my life, when I reminisce about these important events of my life, it becomes clear to me that God was taking care of me by leading me to a perfect wife and mother for my children. Carolyn had deep love and faith in me because during the first two years of our married life we moved fourteen times, living in cheap furnished apartments while I participated in the engineering training program of the oil company that employed me. During the third year of our married life, I changed jobs and went to work for a different oil company. At that time we were living in Bartlesville, Oklahoma and were the proud parents of a three month old baby girl, Barbara Ann. With my new job we were immediately transferred to Ardmore, Oklahoma. Carolyn, Barbara and I drove to that new job in and old car in a snow storm. We were young and not thinking about God helping us, but He was keeping us safe and helping us find our way to a new and better life. There was also deep unconditional love and faith ever present between the three of us and Faith for God as we went about our new adventure. Carolyn certainly showed her love and faith in me during these times. In less than one year we were transferred to another city, Wichita Falls, Texas. With little planning our son, Bill, was born in slightly less than two years after his sister Barbara. God had blessed us with two healthy, beautiful children.

We did not know or think about fear at that young age and time in our lives, although we were continually being blessed with unconditional love from God.

Where, when and why do we depart from the very simple and basic acknowledgements and expressions of unconditional love and Faith? It must be when we begin to experience the emotions of fear, anger and desire along with the emotions of hate, craving and anxiety. When these negative emotions begin to replace the positive emotions of love, joy and peace, which are the emotions found in unconditional love and Faith, our consciousness begins to get mixed up and we become aggressive, selfish and possibly even vengeful. Childhood and early adulthood innocence is a beautiful feeling and a wonderful emotion, but our way of life as human beings seems to cause us to change and become cautious and suspicious, thus losing much of our earlier unconscious and natural emotions of unconditional love and faith with which we were born.

For us to begin to accept and understand the emotions and beliefs involved with unconditional faith in other people and Faith in God and the interrelationship between unconditional love and Faith, it is my belief that we must review, study and analyze our acceptance of Jesus Christ and God as our Lord and Savior. Can our Christian Faith in God and our faith in other persons be separated as two different kinds of faith?

Early on, in our lives when we go to Sunday school and Church, and begin studying the Bible, my belief is that it is easy and natural for us to have reservations regarding many of the Bible Scriptures about Creation and Heaven. I know that I did. In this regard, I remember what became a life changing experience for me. This occurred when I was nine years old participating in a communicants class at church. My dad was building a cow barn with my help when I asked him about Creation and Heaven. My dad answered, as an explanation, by asking me the question: "Why not accept what the Bible teaches until you find a better explanation." For me this early lesson in Believing became a major part of the foundation for my Christian Beliefs. Later on, I learned that in order to become a true Believer, I had to accept God, Jesus Christ and the Holy Spirit unconditionally or find a better explanation. Only through my complete acceptance of unconditional Faith in and love for God could I become a true Christian Believer.

More About My Experiences and Beliefs

My experience and sincere Belief is that becoming a true Christian Believer does not happen for us until we turn everything in our lives over to God. We must make the personal decision to let God do all the leading and that we as individuals do the following. This did not happen quickly for me, nor do I believe it normally happens quickly for anyone. We profess outwardly regarding our Faith as good Christians by going to church regularly and doing all the "right" things. But, in doing all those things outwardly we may not be fully dedicating the complete management of our entire life and all of our activities to the hands of God and Jesus Christ through prayer and acknowledgement that He is all powerful and controls not only each of us individually, but everyone and everything in the universe. It has taken me my entire life to fully begin to understand and accept the fact that to truly live a Godly Christian life we must turn everything over to our Lord God and Jesus Christ. Once we fully understand and accept unconditional love and Faith in God and Jesus Christ as a way of life and turn our lives over to Him to run, life becomes easy. It certainly did for me.

My early Christian teachings have taught me to live a good Christian life, which I have done by trying my best to live by the ten commandments, and by being loyal and trusting to my wives, Carolyn and Donna, and to my family and my friends. And, by being honest and trustworthy in all of my dealings with people both personally and when representing the corporations which employed me. As a child I attended a confirmation class at the First Methodist Church in Bartlesville, Oklahoma, which is now the Bartlesville First Church, a

United Methodist Community and is where we are members. I was nine years old, almost ten, when, at the conclusion of this confirmation class, I was baptized on April 4,1937. I remember the pastor who baptized me, his name was Rev. Broom and he was a very tall lanky man. This confirmation class which culminated in my baptism was a very meaningful experience for me. In remembering that experience and its affect on my life, it was not only meaningful for me, but the lessons taught there and the baptism ceremony established a pattern for my life beliefs, love for God and Christian way of living.

Carolyn and I taught our children Christian beliefs at home and through regular attendance at Sunday school and Church. And, they gave themselves to our Lord God and Jesus Christ with baptism following their communicants classes much as Carolyn and I had done as children.

My employment took us to London when our children were in grade school and junior high school. After three years in London, I was offered a transfer to Columbia as country manager. But, there was no American high school in Bogota, Columbia. Barbara Ann and Bill C. would need to go to a boarding school back home. God knew what was best for me and my family and must have nudged me into turning that offer down. Shortly thereafter the company transferred me back to their home office in Bartlesville were my children could finish high school in a good American school with there former friends. God showed his love and faith in me and my family by directing me to turn down that promotion to Columbia.

God has directed me and answered my prayers many times, but when my young daughter, Barbara died and went to be with God in Heaven I never received an answer from Him as to "why" He took her. He knows that I prayed more than enough asking Him "why" He took her. Barbara had finished her college education with an advanced degree, and had been married about eighteen months. She had been teaching for a year at Westville high school, when she was the victim in a very bad auto accident which took her life. We Christians are taught not to question God's will, that He always has a good plan for each of us. But, at that stage of my life and dedication to God, I could not help but question His wisdom. He has never answered my "why". Carolyn gave me some solace. She was a true Christian Believer, and told me that she believed God took Barbara to Heaven to protect her from future heart aches and sorrows. Carolyn had lost her sister from diabetes complications and she herself had contended with diabetes for many years. She expressed her concern that Barbara or her babies might have diabetes as Carolyn's family carried the diabetes DNA. Maybe this was God's way of helping Carolyn with her grief and through her, my grief. We certainly learned that we should not question God's wisdom even though we do not understand His will or His plans.

In January 1990 when God called Carolyn to be with Him in Heaven, the question of "why" never entered my mind. Possibly, that was because I had learned that God does not answer that question and also because Carolyn was ready for God's call. Her beliefs in God and Jesus were very strong and devout. She was a very quiet person and did not express her devotion outwardly very much. Carolyn had suffered from Type 1 diabetes for over twenty five years, and had spent her last three years with kidney failure and home dialysis, and then suffered a stroke which could not be treated because of her kidney failure. She gave up and God took her to heaven on January 19,1990. Few people, including our close friends, knew of her medical problems because she always kept them to herself. She truly knew the meaning of and practiced unconditional love and Faith both for God and people. My message from God after Carolyn's passing was on March 6,1990 when I was awakened in the middle of the night seeing a vision of Carolyn floating upward above me into a cloud as she was saying "good bye" several times. God often does wonderful things for us. This vision and departing "good bye" gave me comfort and Faith that God would care for her and that He loves her and each of us.

A New Life

In the fall of the year after Carolyn's passing, I started occasionally visiting with the receptionist at the bank I used. I learned her name was Donna Kaye (Morrison) Elam, she was very attractive and I learned that she was divorced and single, so I suggested we have dinner sometime. It took a third try before we actually had a date. I had a conflict the first try, she had family come to town on the second, and on the third try we had dinner at a bar-b-que restaurant. After another few dates we were going steady and I gave her an engagement ring for Christmas. We were married March 4,1991 in Dallas, Texas in the First Presbyterian Church pastor's study by their senior pastor, the Rev. Will Carl III, whom we knew because he had grown up in our home town of Bartlesville. In attendance were my son Bill and his wife Elizabeth, Donna's twin sister Dixie Allen and her husband Ben, and our close friends Bill and Janelle Boyce. We all stayed at the Mansion on Turtle Creek and celebrated with a noon wedding luncheon there following our morning wedding, The following day Donna and I flew to Hawaii for a two week honeymoon.

Donna had many life experiences that severely tested her love and Faith in God. She was married for nearly thirty years to her high school sweetheart when he decided that he wanted free from her and asked for a divorce. Counseling from their pastor did not help because their pastor believed that they should get back together, which was absolutely impossible when her trust in another person for unconditional love and Faith had been completely broken and severed. Donna ended up divorcing him and agreeing to no financial settlement because she was unwilling to fight in court with someone she had loved for what was rightfully hers. She had complete Faith in God, that he would take care of her. And God did take good care of her by giving her a beautiful personality of loving and caring for people. In addition to this loving personality, God gave Donna a very keen sense of knowing when someone could or might be unfaithful or untrustworthy. Her devotion of unconditional love and Faith in God and allowing Him to lead her through life were Donna's greatest assets.

Donna Kaye loved sports, especially basketball in which she excelled during high school. She was often the high point scorer on the Ochelata basketball team which was mentioned several times in our local newspaper "back when" column. She was good enough at basketball to be offered a college scholarship, but decided to marry her high school sweetheart instead. She thoroughly enjoyed watching sports on TV and following our Oklahoma State teams. And, when the NBA Thunder basketball team came to Oklahoma City, she became one of their loyalist fans.

Donna loved to dance, she was a excellent dancer, we particularly enjoyed country and western dancing, going to at least one, maybe two dances a week. We loved to do the Western and Texas two step. And we both liked to line dance. My stroke in May 2008 curtailed our dancing, but we were back to doing some dancing before her stroke. Donna participated in a line dance class once or twice a week. She also enjoyed Tai Chi and participated in those classes a couple of times a week. She was very outgoing and loved being with people.

Donna's brother, J.R., was a retired marine veteran, having served in three wars. During his overseas service in the Vietnam war, his wife ran off with another man, abandoning and leaving their small children to be cared for by others. Donna took care of and raised J.R.'s daughter from childhood to an adult. After Donna's and my marriage, although J.R.'s daughter was grown and married with children of her own, she and her family became like a daughter and family to both of us. Donna and I loved and cared for them as we would have cared for our own children. Later on, in addition to helping her brother in this way and following his becoming an alcoholic, Donna sponsored J.R. through the Alcoholics Anonymous twelve step program. With her loving help through the AA program, he recovered and never relapsed into drinking again. Donna always practiced unselfish, unconditional love and Faith wherever and whenever she was needed.

Cooking was Donna's passion and she was very good at everything she did in the kitchen. She loved to bake a chocolate cake or a batch of cookies and take it to someone she knew or to the staff whenever we went to a dance, to a doctor or dentist office, have a car serviced or anywhere else there might be a group of people. She was known for her delicious chocolate cakes. Several women friends have asked me for her recipe, but it was in her head, she never wrote it down. She fixed meals for anyone that she learned needed a meal. An older lady and retired school teacher, Della Craighead, did not like to cook and Donna prepared and took her meals several times a week for eight or nine years. Donna's brother, J.R. would run out of money frequently toward the end of the month and Donna would take him meals. She did her own "meals on wheels" for anybody she learned needed help.

In addition to the every day baking and preparing meals, Donna loved to host dinner parties, she loved to entertain both family and friends. She loved the Christmas season. Donna Kaye always decorated our home beautifully, but the Christmas season was special because it represented the birth of Jesus our savior and we wanted our home to be extra pretty for Him at that time. We decorated for Christmas just before Thanksgiving because we nearly always entertained all of both her and my families at our home for Thanksgiving dinner. Another tradition that we practiced every year for over twenty years was a big Christmas dinner party for our families and close friends. This usually involved about sixty guests and Donna would plan, organize and cook beautiful meals for these dinner parties. Her last one of these beautiful Christmas dinner parties was only a week before her debilitating stroke, it was on December 15, 2012. In addition to being our annual Christmas dinner party, it was her brother, Frank's ninetieth birthday. He came to our party from Edmond, Oklahoma, and his son, grandson and there wives also came from out of town to be there for that dinner party. It was a grand affair, we entertained about twenty five family members and thirty five close friends. Donna was doing what she loved to do, and she did it beautifully. God was always with her and helping her.

Our New Home

From Donna's and my marriage in 1991 we lived in a large two story home which was nearly twenty five years old. About that time we began talking and thinking about sizing down and eliminating maintenance and repair with a new home. Our neighbor was developing a small subdivision with small lots and we picked out one of his best lots for building our new home. Some of my earlier experience and work included designing houses, and after spending well over one hundred hours designing a house for this lot, my neighbor switched lots on me. While stopping by his new subdivision one day, and visiting with him, he informed me that the lot we were looking at and talking about building on, was not our lot, our lot was another lot, which appeared to be one of the worst lots in the subdivision. We had not signed a contract or paid down any money, so there was no problem backing out of the deal. Not more than a week later my neighbor started building a house on the lot we had spoken for, for his golfing buddy. Although this seemed to be very disappointing at the time, God must have been there guiding us in a better direction. In discussing this situation with my friend and builder, Victor Jones, who had built, maintained, and added on to our first home, he suggested considering the Starview subdivision across the road from the one in which we had been involved earlier. This subdivision was going to be a more upscale subdivision with larger more spacious lots and larger houses. We finalized our new home plans with Victor Jones building us a beautiful home in the Starview addition. Donna and I have, on many occasions, thanked God for His intervention in our planning a new home by giving us so much more than we were looking for. We will never know if this was only a simple misunderstanding, or if God was truly at work directing us to something much better. In our new home, we designed and built a spacious kitchen for Donna where she could fully enjoy her passion for cooking and entertaining.

Donna's Influence

I never became even close to recognizing and expressing how to be truly unconditional in my Faith and love for God until my wife Donna taught me the meaning of this wonderful way of life and beautiful conscious emotion. She showed me how to live and love through her unconditional love for and Faith in God and in me. She taught me Faith in God by her daily study of the Bible and beautiful, loving Christian life style. I am truly and deeply indebted to Donna for teaching me so much about love and Faith through her Christian life style example. We both loved God and Jesus Christ unconditionally and believed in Him as our Lord and Savior.

Donna cared for me as a mother does for her baby when I was stricken with a stroke in May 2008. My stroke came on slowly, starting on a Friday evening with only slight dizziness, but not bad enough to put me down, Saturday was uneventful and we went to church that Sunday, but by Monday I needed help to walk. Monday morning we went to Dr. Brownings office in Tulsa, and as I walked in using a cane, he said "Bill you are having a stroke". He immediately sent me to a neurologist, who diagnosed my stroke as being in the right cerebellum part of my brain, and then called for CT's and MRI's twice to confirm his diagnosis. By that time I needed a wheel chair to get around. The two doctors prescribed for me the blood thinner Plavix and decided that it would be better for me to stay at home with 24 hour home nursing care than to go into a hospital. They were concerned about falls and the risk of breaking a hip in a hospital. Donna anxiously agreed to oversee caring for me at home. I spent about three weeks in bed and using a wheel chair with 24hour home nursing care and with Donna overseeing my care. After that Donna took over and cared for me with day time home nursing help. Although I was wheel chair bound for another two or three months, Donna took great care of me at home and by taking me daily to out patient physical therapy at Jane Phillips Hospital for speech, arms and hands occupational therapy, and to physical therapy for my legs and body. This outpatient physical therapy went on daily for nearly six months until I was able to walk comfortably with a cane. Physical therapy continued after that two or three times a week with Donna helping me at home with supporting exercises. About eighteen months after my stroke, Donna and I were beginning to go dancing a little. Jane Phillips Hospital then wanted to publicize my good recovery by taking the following photo of us dancing and using this photo in a poster about the hospital's good quality of care, close to home. This poster hung in the hospital lobby for almost four years until it was brought to Donna's room where she was confined from her stroke. The hospital poster did not recognize that Donna's unconditional love and Faith in God and me was possibly the most important factor to my recovery. My unconditional love and Faith in God and Donna were there also. But, most importantly, God was always there with us and for us because we both had complete Faith that God would take care of us. While all of my stroke recovery was going on, we were building our new home, and Donna was loaded with much decision making for our new home while caring for me. We would never have survived without God's full time help, and our deep devotion to unconditional love and faith for each other and for our sincere and deep love and Faith in God and Jesus Christ.

Donna and Bill Dancing after Bill's Stroke

Unconditional "People" faith and "God" Faith

Unconditional faith in and between two people is a very interesting phenomenon. Truly unconditional faith between two people becomes much like love for and Faith in God which may be the very basis for accepting and practicing unconditional love and faith between two people. Unconditional love and faith becomes accepting and loving another person without reservations of any kind and accepting them as they are without judgement. In many ways, Faith in our Lord God and Jesus Christ equates to these same emotions that occur between people, but with much deeper and more meaningful involvement in our Beliefs and convictions. When we consider that "unconditional" means without any, absolutely no reservations or conditions about Faith, we must accept that we would have to be absolutely and completely without sin to have and practice unconditional Faith. The Bible teaches us that abstinence from sin is unattainable because no one is ever completely free from sin. Only Jesus was and is without sin. And only Jesus can forgive our sins, thus removing all of our sins from us. If we were able to free ourselves of sin by ourselves without asking for Jesus' help, we would have reached perfection. Thus absolute unconditional Faith and love in our Lord God and Jesus Christ would be perfection. We will only reach perfection when we die and all our sins are forgiven by Jesus. However, in the meantime we can work diligently toward loving, forgiving, and living by the ten commandments as Jesus taught during his life time. Maybe by living our lives with conscious love and faith in and for other human beings, we can come closer to living a life of unconditional Faith and love for our Lord God and Jesus Christ. And in so doing, maybe, just maybe we could approach perfection. We could certainly improve our world here on earth greatly and make all our lives a lot better, as well as make our earth a much better place in which to live. My mom and dad, my first wife, Carolyn, and our children, Barbara Ann and Bill C. all provided me with unconditional love and Faith during my early life with them. When we are young we do not think much about these emotions and Beliefs, but in retrospect they were always there for us and were very important to our lives. My early immediate family gave me the roots for a lifetime of unconditional love and Faith in God and in my family. My essay relates a few of our family experiences with God taking very good care of us by helping us make decisions to do what was best for us, especially during our our times of need.

On a continuing basis each of us experiences an inside and an outside to our lives. On the outside we protect our internal life, our intimacy, our loved ones, and our personal beliefs. We tend to share one face with the outer world, while at the same time keeping watch that nothing penetrates the sanctity of our internal peace. From inside our brains we have many ways to look at the outer world, but we only open up to those we trust. God is always there to help us identify mutual trust, if we listen to Him. We need to learn to better practice unconditional love and trust for others like God always does for us. In our relationships with fellow human beings it becomes necessary that unconditional love and faith become an absolutely honest two way interchange between and among us for there to be complete trust and love. All persons involved must express and experience the conscious emotions of unconditional love and faith in and for each other as well as for their love and Faith in God.

In studying about faith with a capital letter "F" honoring our Faith in God and Jesus Christ, our greatest gift from God is His absolute and unconditional love and Faith in each of us, both individually and personally. Our Faith in God should personify our belief that He loves us unconditionally by forgiving our sins and accepting us as His children, unconditionally. God sets for us the exquisite example and standard for measuring unconditional love by the way He loves us and continually cares for each of us. There is no need for any further example or definition of unconditional love, for God's love for each of us is perfection. If only, we as individuals, could constantly emulate the same unconditional love and Faith in Him as our Lord and Savior as He does in each of us, we would truly be Saved.

God's Communication with Us

This attention to unconditional love and Faith brings to my mind the question of just how does God communicate his love and Faith in and for us, to us. In my study and analysis of this subject, I found one very outstanding reference: Rev. Adam Hamilton, in his book "Making Sense of the Bible" has an excellent chapter on how God speaks to us and through us. He acknowledges that hearing an audible voice, although not impossible, seems at most very unusual. Rev. Hamilton describes his experiences of hearing God as "a flash of insight, a gentile persistent nudge, or occasionally as a conversation in his head". Others I have talked to about hearing from God describe their hearing from God in similar ways. My experience has been much the same, that I have an emotional experience or feeling coming from my heart, mind and body telling me what I should do or that everything is all right.

One of my experiences of hearing from God was with regard to writing this essay. I had many reservations holding me back and keeping me from beginning to write. One day, as I was praying about whether or not to start writing, I had an emotional experience telling me to go ahead and start, that He would help me. So here I am, writing about love and Faith, for which I have no writing experience, but am writing from my heart with God's help. And, amazingly, I have been able to express myself in unbelievable ways. There is no way I could be writing this alone, God must be helping me. Any expertise I have in writing was learned from engineering, technical and policy types of writing. This essay can only have come from my heart with God's help.

My use of the word "observed" in the title of this essay "Unconditional Love and Faith Observed" was chosen because of my familiarity with C. S. Lewis' book "A Grief Observed". I believe the word "observed" correctly and accurately describes and expresses very well the content of both his book and my essay. Lewis' descriptions of his experiences with grief regarding his wife are wonderful and they very eloquently express many of the same emotions and feelings of grief that I have experienced from both Carolyn's and Donna's passing. But my experiences of loving and loosing my dear wives dictates that I remember, think about, and write about the more positive side of my experiences and memories with regard to love, joy, peace and Faith.

My Poem about Donna Kaye's True Love

Shortly after Donna Kaye went to be with our Lord, I decided to write a poem about her regarding her deep devotion to God and love for people. Writing poetry never was my calling, but with God's help I was able to write the following tribute to her. My poem is titled "True Love" because that was her true belief and feeling for life. And, in remembrance of her love for God and people, I arranged for "True Love Knows No Bounds" to be engraved as the epitaph on her tomb stone. Donna loved God first and foremost and then she loved people, the world and everything in it. She loved to welcome people where ever she was and to make them feel comfortable. She was always telling me she loved God first and me more, and I would counter that I loved her more.

True Love

True Love Knows No Bounds

Donna truly loved our Lord God first and foremost.
She often told me that she loved God first and
she never forgot her Faith in Him.

True Love Knows No Bounds

She truly loved me too, and often told me so.
She frequently told me that she loved me more every day,
and I often told her I loved her more every day too.

True Love Knows No Bounds

God blessed Donna and me by bringing us together in true love.
He gave us 22 years of wonderful, loving togetherness
for which we are forever truly grateful.

True Love Knows No Bounds

She loved people without regard to their background
and was always ready to help anyone in need.
Her will to help and comfort people focused
on family, the elderly and sick.

True Love Knows No Bounds

Donna was truly the love of my life.
I told her so, for everyone to hear, at my 85th birthday party,
and she loved hearing me say this.

True Love Knows No Bounds

She nursed and cared for me lovingly for nearly five
years following my stroke.
God only allowed me to nurse and care for her for six
months following her stroke. The doctors and I did everything we
possibly could to help God nurse her back to good health.

True Love Knows No Bounds

Donna truly loved the roses I grew for her.
From early spring to late fall each year, I cut roses for her
every morning to show my love for her and for us to begin each day.

True Love Knows No Bounds

Donna loved her family always fulfilling their needs, both large and small.
She frequently observed and filled their needs without being asked.

True Love Knows No Bounds

Donna loved my son, Bill C., and his family as she did her own family.
My son Bill was a God send to Donna and me during these
trying times, he was always there to help and comfort when needed.
And he continues to regularly check on and comfort me in my grief.

True Love Knows No Bounds

She deeply loved her niece, Judy, who she raised as a child.
We both love Judy and her family like she was our own daughter and family.
Judy loved Donna too and often helped care for her during her illness.

True Love Knows No Bounds

Donna loved her new home and kitchen and
thoroughly enjoyed preparing meals, cooking for and
entertaining family and friends in her home.

True Love Knows No Bounds

Donna always loved and cared for me through sickness
and in health, never wavering in her true love for me.

True Love Knows No Bounds

She never forgot that she truly loved God first and foremost, and she
prayed constantly for Him to guide and help her.
In her relationships with everyone, she always acted with humility
and tried never to offend anyone.

True Love Knows No Bounds

She deeply loved her twin sister Dixie and always catered
to Dixie's desires, for Dixie was the dominate twin and liked to control Donna.

True Love Knows No Bounds

Donna loved Christmas and always made it the big event of the year
for both family and friends.
Her Christmas dinner parties were beautiful and the delight
of everyone, her parties really could not have been out done.

True Love Knows No Bounds

One of Donna's cooking specialities was her delicious chocolate cakes,
which everyone loved, and she loved making and giving away.
She frequently arose at 5:30 a.m. and had a
chocolate cake baked and ready for someone special before I arose.

True Love Knows No Bounds

Donna loved to study natural health and was very
knowledgeable about vitamins, diet and exercise.
She worked diligently at good health and exercise for herself
and enjoyed helping others achieve natural good health

True Love Knows No Bounds

Donna is in Heaven now with our Lord God and Jesus the Christ,
always and truly her first and foremost love.
She most certainly has a Crown of Glory in Heaven for
her everlasting loving goodness and kindness while here on earth.

True Love Knows No Bounds

Bill Belknap July 2013

I truly believe God inspired me to write this poem to honor Donna Kaye in this way for her love of God, people and life. She was a blessing to everyone she knew and came in contact with by always living and showing all the love, trust, Faith and other attributes that Jesus teaches us. Donna truly lived a Godly life and is dearly missed by all.

DONNA KAYE'S TOMB STONE

When selecting and designing Donna's tomb stone, I included the epitaph: "True Love Knows No Bounds" to recognize her spirit of love for God, everyone and everything. The epitaph "True Love Knows No Bounds" was my personal inspiration to describe Donna Kaye's life style and beliefs. She so beautifully, consciously and consistently lived according to 1 Corinthians 13:4-7 (NRSV) that this Bible verse describes her perfectly:

> "Love is patient; love is kind; love is not envious or boastful or arrogant or rude. It does not insist on its own way; it is not irritable or resentful; it does not rejoice in wrong doing, but rejoices in the truth. It bears all things, believes all things, hopes all things, endures all things."

Donna Kaye not only lived by, but often quoted this scripture. She certainly lived by it, and in so doing encouraged everyone around her to also live according to this scripture.

Following is a photograph of Donna's tomb stone showing her epitaph. The two crosses acknowledge both of our beliefs in God and Jesus Christ, the heart with the number 22 on it acknowledges our 22 years of beautiful wedded life, and the two roses represent the roses I grew and cut for her each summer morning. Donna's body now rests in the Ochelata, Oklahoma Cemetery, in the Morrison family plot with her parents and brother, J.R. I will join her there soon.

Donna's Tomb Stone

DAILY BIBLE STUDY

My daily routine includes a morning devotional of reading and studying the Bible, the reference I currently use is the "One Year Bible". This book for studying the the Bible was given to me by my close friend, Jene Dewey, while Donna was sick. It includes passages for each day of the year from each of four parts of the Bible: the Old Testament, the New Testament, Psalms, and Proverbs. On the morning of December 4th, 2014 my New Testament lesson was: 1 John 4:1-21. There I was on that day a technical writer trying my best to write about love and Faith, with very deep convictions about these subjects, and God shows me these beautiful Bible verses about love. Believe it or not, I was exactly at this point in my writing on December 4, 2014 when these Bible verses were referenced in my daily devotional lesson. God certainly has His own ways of speaking to us. In my studying and analyzing love there does not seem to be any better description of the interrelationships between God's love for us, our love for Him and our love each other. Quoted below is this wonderful, beautiful scripture about God's love for us and the way we should love Him: 1 John 4: 7-21 (NRSV):

"Beloved, let us love one another, because love is from God; and whoever loves has been of God and knows God. Everyone who loves is born of God and knows God. Whoever does not love does not know God, for God is love. God's love was revealed among us in this way: God sent his only son into the world so that we might live through him. In this is love, not that we loved God but that He loved us and sent his Son to be the atoning sacrifice for our sins. Beloved, since God loved us so much, we also ought to love one another. No one has ever seen God; if we love one another, God lives in us and his love is perfected in us.

By this we know that we abide in him and he in us, because he has given us his Spirit. And we have seen and do testify that the Father has sent His Son to be Savior of the world. God abides in those who confess that Jesus is the Son of God, and they abide in God. So we have known and believe the love that God has for us.

God is love, and and those who abide in love abide in God, and God abides in them. Love has been perfected among us in this: that we may have boldness on the day of judgment, because as he is, so are we in this world. There is no fear in love, but perfect love casts out fear; for fear has to do with punishment, and whoever fears has not reached perfection in love. We love because he first loved us. Those who say, "I love God" and hate their brothers, are liars; for those who do not love a brother or sister whom they have seen, cannot love God whom they have not seen. The commandment we have from him is this: Those who love God must love their brothers and sisters also."

These verses of Biblical Scripture so very accurately and vividly describe Donna Kaye's beliefs and her way of life that they needed to be quoted here and referenced as to how they came to my attention. They express accurately and beautifully both Donna's and my sincere Belief in God, His love for us and our love for Him, and for our need to love one another.

Bartlesville First Church Memorial to Donna Kaye Belknap

O ur new Church building and property needed a sign at the front of our property to identify it and invite people into Church. Our pastors approached me with the idea of giving and dedicating such a sign as a memorial to Donna Kaye because of her regular and consistently gracious greeting and welcoming of everyone to Church services, functions and meetings. This idea appealed to me and resulted in the beautiful sign we now have at Bartlesville First Church inviting and welcoming everyone to God's place for worship. A photograph of our sign at the time of it's dedication is included following my dedication words.

My Memorial Sign Dedication

This Memorial Sign welcoming people to Bartlesville First Church is a very fitting Memorial to my wife Donna Kaye Belknap because she enjoyed welcoming everyone into church any time she was here, but especially on Sunday mornings during our welcoming periods as we began worship. Donna and I normally sat near the back of the church because of my stroke, and she would walk down the center isle greeting everyone with a friendly hand shake and big smile, making them feel comfortable and welcome. I think our pastor Dr. Kevin Tully would wait for her to get to the alter rail to end the welcoming. Donna really knew about and exactly what unconditional love meant and she practiced showing love continually everywhere she went with everyone she met. Donna loved people and always wanted them to feel welcome wherever she was. This sign will certainly announce our Church's presence and welcome people to Bartlesville First Church as a memorial to her. I am very happy and pleased to be able to do this for First Church as a memorial to my loving wife Donna Kaye Belknap.

Bill Belknap, June 8, 2014

Donna's Memorial Church Sign

The Cornerstone, our church's monthly news publication, presents a very nice article about Donna Kaye's sign and her dedication service for the sign. Not only does this particular issue of Cornerstone feature the sign and dedication, but it explains the significance of Pentecost Sunday, which was the Sunday of Donna's memorial sign dedication. We should always remember that Pentecost is the day on which Christian churches commemorate the coming of the Holy Spirit into the hearts of the apostles and others assembled in Jerusalem. And that Pentecost celebrates the beginning of the Christian church and the promulgation of Christianity everywhere. Pentecost Sunday was the perfect time for the dedication of our church sign and to remember Donna Kaye for her evangelism of welcoming everyone to and making them comfortable in church with her beautiful smile and hand shake. The front page of the Cornerstone showing the sign dedication is copied below:

BARTLESVILLE FIRST CHURCH

Ephesians 2:19-20: You are members of God's household, with Christ Jesus himself as the chief

CORNERSTONE

June 11, 2014 · Editor: desira.mathes@bartlesvillefirstchurch.com

Pentecost

Pentecost is one of the principal days of the Christian year, celebrated on the fiftieth day after Easter. The Greek word pentecoste means "fiftieth day."

Pentecost is the day on which the Christian church commemorates the coming of the Holy Spirit upon the apostles and others assembled in Jerusalem. It marks the beginning of the Christian church and the proclamation of its message throughout the world and is often referred to as the birthday of the church. The liturgical color for Pentecost is red.

Traditionally, Pentecost has been a day for baptisms. Because it was the custom in the early church for persons being baptized to wear white robes or clothing, the day also became known as Whitsunday, a contraction of white Sunday.

It's More Than Just a New Sign

It's more than just a new sign, it's a new way to welcome the community.

Designed and installed by Image Builders of Owasso, First Church's new monument sign stands at over 20 feet tall and features a full-color LED video display as its centerpiece.

The sign was dedicated to the memory of longtime church member Donna Kaye Belknap. Her husband Bill says welcoming was what Donna did best.

"Donna loved to welcome people everywhere she was," Bill said. "She loved people, she loved the unconditionally and, at church in particular, whatever church event it was, she was always there welcoming people.

"At Sunday services…she loved to go down that center aisle, shaking hands with everyone, giving them that big, beautiful smile."

Through memorials like this one, people's influence can live on long after they're gone.

"It seems so appropriate because of Donna's lovely way of welcoming people." Bill concluded. "The sign will welcome people, she loved to welcome people to the church, and it will be a beautiful memorial for her."

Church Paper About Memorial Sign

♦ 30 ♦

DONNA KAYE LOVED COMMUNION

Donna Kaye's favorite church service was always Communion. She loved to go to church on Communion Sundays and tried to always attend church on those Sundays. She felt very close to God and Jesus during Communion services, and because of her unconditional love and Faith in God and Jesus she taught me to understand and experience the same beautiful feelings of unconditional love and Faith in Him, especially during Communion. Now without Donna, my participation in Communion Services is heartbreaking for me, even though I know God is right there with me, Donna is missing.

Additional Experiences With God's Communications and Help

Earlier I discussed how I believe God communicates with us, referencing Rev. Adam Hamilton's description: "a flash of insight, a gentle persistent nudge, or occasionally as a conversation in his head". This quote from Rev. Hamilton's book accurately describes my experiences of believing God has communicated something to me. I have already described my experiences of hearing God encourage me regarding my decision to write this essay, His help while writing my poem about Donna, and His timing for my reading of 1 John 4:7-21 while writing this essay.

Another time I heard from God occurred after praying many times for Donna to, in some way, tell me or let me know how she was doing in Heaven. On this occasion God answered my prayer through a message from her. This communication occurred while I was walking on my tread mill one morning, not even thinking about God or Donna, I was suddenly aware that Donna was telling me that she was OK and not to worry about her. This was very heart warming for me and immediately afterwards I felt a very serene and peaceful silence come over me. This experience was a great help and comfort to me in my grief journey for Donna.

The subject of communicating with God is very difficult for me to write about because I do not want to overstate or understate my experiences, nor do I want to seem to be in any way clairvoyant about what has been experienced. I am trying my best, with God's help, to tell my experiences exactly as they occurred. My belief is that I have not listened closely enough in the past for God's word when He was communicating something to me. Following several of these experiences, I seem to have a better understanding and appreciation for how quietly God works on His own time table, and I am much more sensitive to looking for and observing His beckoning.

A very rewarding experience of my hearing from God occurred this past December, before Christmas. Having frequently prayed to God for Donna to tell me about Heaven, I was blessed with the gift of a book titled "Heaven" by Randy Alcorn. This book was a Christmas gift from a couple who have been close friends for many years. They are devout Christians and students of the Bible. But, they had no idea and no way of knowing that I had been praying for Donna to tell me about Heaven.

Alcorn's book is a documentary from the Bible pulling together all of the scripture that describes Heaven as God must intend it to be. In the words from this book: "Heaven is a bright, vibrant, and physical New Earth, free from sin, suffering, and death, and brimming with Jesus Christ's presence, wondrous natural beauty, and the richness of human culture as God intended". God answered my prayer and gave me a continuing challenge for studying His word from the Bible with new knowledge and assistance from this book.

This experience of wanting to know about Heaven, asking God for help and then receiving His help has been an absolutely wonderful experience for me. God does know our needs and He does answer our prayers. All we need to do is acknowledge and accept the fact that He is our Lord and supreme leader, and turn everything over to Him. He will take care of us.

All of my experiences of seeing God at work and of His answering prayers are not recent. Earlier in this essay, events undoubtedly directed by God were described. Most of those events occurred before my learning to look more closely for and to acknowledge God's help.

In June 1978, God answered my prayers in a very powerful way. At that time I was living in Teheran, Iran working as the Middle East Regional Manager of a major Oil Company and country manager for Iran. The political climate was tense in Iran, but did not seem serious. I was privileged to have lunch monthly with Iran's American Ambassador, Richard Helms, who had very privately advised those of us who lunched with him regularly, that the Shaw was in poor health. Ambassador Helms knew the Shaw of Iran personally because he had attended boarding school with him in Switzerland. Because of several assassinations of Americans in preceding years, the Embassy was armoring their cars and taking other security precautions. Ambassador Helms recommended that we follow established security practices including not going back and forth to work at the same times or using the same routes every day and to be very alert to possible terrorist activity. At that time, I had experienced two telephoned bomb threats on my house, neither of which occurred. Because of the assassination of four TRW employees riding in a jeep in late 1977, the security situation had become much more tense during the spring of 1978.

The oil company for which I worked had discovered huge natural gas reserves in the Bandar Abbas area of southern Iran and we had been working for over three years on a very extensive and expensive project to compress and liquify this natural gas and export liquid gas to Japan. Our contractual agreement with Iran was very explicit and detailed about oil, but very week regarding ownership and development of natural gas. Consequently, we had to renegotiate a revised deal to develop and sell the natural gas reserves. The Iranian government officials were absolutely unwilling to give the oil company partnership, which I represented, an acceptable internal rate of return (profit) on the huge investment involved for this project. These negotiations had been going on for nearly three years and were getting absolutely nowhere.

Because of my knowledge of the security issues in Iran, I was praying to God daily asking Him for direction regarding what should be done about and for the safety of our American families in Iran. At that time we had about thirty American families living in Iran. Early afternoon, one day in the middle of June 1978, the day before my wife and I were planning to leave Teheran and come home for annual leave, an official of the Iranian Government Oil Company phoned me and ordered that I meet in his office that afternoon at 2:00 p.m. regarding the gas liquefaction project. He insisted on a meeting before I left town. At this meeting he and the other Government officials repeated their same song and dance regarding their position and I repeated our position as outlined previously many times by our partnership in many meetings. I may have rankled or possibly insulted them a little, because I was wearing my prescription sun glasses. In my hurry to get to their meeting, because of the short notice, I had forgotten my regular clear glasses and I was also wearing a casual jeans suit. It was during summer office hours, and I did not have time to go home and change to a business suit. Looking back on and thinking about this meeting, I believe God was setting me up for what happened next regarding our presence in Iran.

The following day my wife, Carolyn, and I left Teheran for our annual leave and came home. The oil company executive vice president that I reported to phoned me as soon as I was in town asking me to meet him in his office the following day. At that meeting he showed me a Telex (which was the way we communicated overseas in 1978) from the Iranian government officials saying that I could not work in Iran any more (persona-non-grata) and insisting that I be replaced because they could not deal with me on the gas liquefaction project. I advised my vice president that all I had done was restate the position set out by our partnership. He was fully aware of the security problems and other concerns in Iran from earlier communications. After consulting with another vice president, he made the decision during this meeting to close the Teheran office, lay off all our local employees, and bring all of our Americans home.

The Teheran office was closed and all of our American families were out of Iran eight to ten months before the Shaw was deposed and the American Embassy taken over by the Moslem opposition in 1979. It is my belief that God was certainly at work saving His people largely because I had prayed for their safety. God, through His direction of all these actions also saved the oil company partnership hundreds of millions of dollars of investment that would have been confiscated by Iran later. Many of my friends with other oil companies lost everything they had in Iran, they were lucky to get out of the country with the shirts on their backs. God is always working for us if we only tell Him our needs through prayer and let Him do everything His way.

Another interesting fact related to this experience is that the executive vice president, who closed our Teheran office and got all our people out of Iran, and his wife were in earlier years, my two young children's Sunday school teachers. God is everywhere and always at work for us.

One time, a long time ago, in reviewing my life with God, I recall a time when God may have been talking to me and I was not listening, did not want to hear, or most likely had not learned to listen. This occurred when I was a freshman in college. The house mother of the victory hall in which I was living, a Mrs. Williams, who was a mature lady, older than my mother, talked to me at least twice about becoming a minister. At that time, preparing for Seminary and entering the Ministry did not interest me at all, my plans were to study engineering and business management and become a corporate executive. What a different life I might have had, if I had been listening when God may have been talking to me through her. However, I have absolutely no regrets, God has lead me through a wonderful, very successful and joyful life for which I am extremely grateful. As I review my life, I can see that God has always been there directing me in how to live through his Word, and helping me to get through the rough times.

Most Recent Word from God

My latest experience of hearing from God, was on January 17, 2015, a Saturday morning when I was home alone, having eaten breakfast, walked on my tread mill, and read my daily Bible lesson, I was sort of day dreaming about living alone and dying alone, feeling sorry for myself. I think Satan was trying to get a hold on me. When out of the blue, I had what might be called a premonition, it seemed that my whole outlook and concept of things changed abruptly and something deep inside me said to me: "Do not worry, Donna will be there". And then a very tranquil, extremely peaceful feeling of God's Presence came over me. God was certainly at work that morning and that experience with God's words has sustained and helped me greatly. It gave me a much brighter outlook about my remaining life. This message from God gave me hope.

DONNA KAYE'S BEAUTY

With her continual outpouring of unconditional love and Faith, Donna Kaye was on earth and is in Heaven a beautiful person inside. In addition to always reflecting her spirit and sole with unconditional love and Faith, she was also just as beautiful to observe on the outside as she was on the inside. And it would be an injustice not to include a photo of her here. A recent photo I really like is from my 85th birthday celebration on August 18, 2012, when I told her and everyone there that she was the love of my life. My daughter-in-law, Elizabeth, took this photo of Donna Kaye looking at me when I was speaking those words. Donna was looking at me in this photo with that very beautiful look in her eyes of unconditional love and faith for me. You can see we shared deep feelings of truly unconditional love and faith for each other as well as Faith for God our Lord and Savior.

Donna at Bill's 85th Birthday Party

Another photo of Donna which I love and is my favorite was taken during our twentieth wedding anniversary celebration. Elizabeth also took this photo. And, we used this photo for Donna's Memorial Services and for the photo on her Memorial Church Sign for it's dedication.

Donna at 20th Wedding Anniversary

ADVENT LOVE CANDLE LIGHTING

During this past Christmas season the lighting of the Advent candle for Love touched my heart and Spirit deeply. Since Love, Joy and Peace are our consciousness' path to Enlightenment, unconditional Love becomes the first and most important step in attaining our desired relationship with God. I quote from the ceremony of lighting the forth and Love Advent candle: The candles of Hope and Peace had been lighted already in remembrance that Christ will come again to fulfill all of God's promises and to bring Peace and Joy to all of us.

"The fourth candle of Advent is the candle of love. God's love is a perfect love. It holds nothing back. God, in love, gives us everything we need to live a life of hope and peace.

The Bible says that "God so loved the world that He gave His only Son, so that whoever believes in Him should not perish, but have eternal life." Jesus shows us God's perfect love.

This is what love is like. Love is patient, love is kind and envies no one. Love is never boastful or conceited, rude or selfish. Love is not quick to take offense, it keeps no records of wrongs, it does not gloat over other peoples troubles, but rejoices in the right, the good, and the true. There is nothing that love cannot face; there is no limit to its Faith, to its hope, to its endurance.

Love never ends. We light the candle of love to remind us that Jesus brings us God's love and shows us how to love others.

Love is like a light shinning in a dark place. As we look at this candle we celebrate the love we find in Jesus Christ."

This description of love by God for us and of our love for God beautifully expresses Donna's beliefs and her way of life. She knew and lived a life of love in the truest sense.

HOPE

In his sermon on that fourth Sunday of Advent, Dr. Tully made the point that "memories bring hope" which caught my attention because so many of our hopes are based on our memories. But, as Dr. Tully observed, we need to separate the hopes that involve material things we may be wishing for, from the Godly hopes that involve love, joy and peace.

In analyzing what hope is all about and how it relates to unconditional love and Faith in God and Jesus Christ, my conclusion is that the ultimate hope of nearly every Christian Believer is to be accepted by our Lord God and to be welcomed into Heaven by Jesus Christ.

HEAVEN

Before writing more about hope, I would like to relate my erudition regarding Heaven. Previously I have conveyed that I often prayed to God for Donna Kaye tell me about Heaven, and how God must have directed my good Christian friends to answer these prayers by giving me Randy Alcorn's book "Heaven" for Christmas. From reading and analyzing his book my opinion is that Alcorn's book on Heaven presents the most beautiful, positive, hopeful outlook regarding our future relationship with God and the Trinity in Heaven that can be imagined. His book is fully documented and based almost entirely on God's word in the Bible. He answers in detail, with Biblical references, every question anyone could possibly think of about Heaven and the New Earth which God has prepared for us. Following is a summation quoted from his book:

"The most ordinary moment on the New Earth will be greater than the most perfect moments in this life---those experiences you wanted to bottle or hang on to but couldn't. It can get better, far better, than this---and it will. Life on the New Earth will be like sitting in front of the fire with family and friends, basking in the warmth, laughing uproariously, dreaming of the adventures to come---and then going out and living those adventures together. With no fear that life will ever end or that tragedy will descend like a dark cloud. With no fear that dreams will be shattered or relationships broken."

To confirm God's promise of Heaven and the New Earth being like Alcorn describes in his summary, he advises that we need only to refer to the apostle John's words in Revelations 21:1,3-5 (NIV):

> "Then I saw a new heaven and a new earth....And I heard a loud voice from the throne saying, "Now the dwelling of God is with men, and He will live with them. They will be His people, and God Himself will be with them and be their God. He will wipe tear from their eyes. There will be no more death or mourning or crying or pain, for the old order of things has passed away." He who was seated on the throne said, "I am making everything new!" Then He said, "Write this down, for these words are trustworthy and true."

Learning more details about what God says in the Bible regarding exactly what Heaven will be like has been a revelation for me, it has given me a much more beautiful and positive view of what life in Heaven and the New World will be like. My oh my, take all the beauty, love and joy we have here and remove all the fear, grief and bad, along with being in the presence of God and Jesus Christ will truly be Heaven.

Hope Eternal

Since my view and sincere belief is that nearly every true Believer"s ultimate hope must be to go to Heaven and to be there with God and Jesus Christ, I would like to expand on this thought from what I learned reading Lewis Smedes book "Keeping Hope Alive". He reviews many situations in true life where hope has been the major factor in bringing about the happening of good things. He ties these actual living experiences into help from God through His answering of prayers. Rev. Smedes sums up his treatise on hope by saying that when God gets involved in our hoping, that hope becomes thrust in Him and the promises He makes to us in the Bible. My analysis is in full and complete agreement with him, no one should ever argue with this philosophy. Rev. Smedes quotes that God promises the following three things in the Bible:

"He promises to be with us even when life tells us that He has abandoned us."
"He promises that His children will live after they die."
"He promises to make our world to work right again"

The lesson or conclusion then becomes that God is frequently our fall back position for hope, but when He gets involved, God is the one who keeps our hope alive. This has been my personal experience, throughout Donna's sickness following her stroke, my only refuge was looking to God and asking for His help with her recovery and hoping that she would get better and ultimately recover.

PRAYER OF HOPE

Since Donna's passing to be with God in Heaven, I have composed a prayer of hope for me to join her in Heaven when that is God's will. This prayer did not come to me suddenly or all at once. With God's help, it evolved over several months of praying for Donna and myself. I believe it expresses my sincere beliefs and feelings about Donna's and my future. I pray this prayer several times daily and believe it will be answered by God when He is willing and ready for me to join Donna Kaye in Heaven.

My Prayer of Hope

Our Father who art in Heaven, hallowed be Thy name.
Thy kingdom come, Thy will be done on earth as it is in Heaven.
Give us this day, our daily bread,
And forgive us our sins, as we forgive those who sin against us.
And lead us not into temptation, but deliver us from evil.
For Thine is the kingdom, and the power and the glory,
forever and ever. Amen, Amen.
Lord, Thank you for all of the many, many blessings with which You have
blessed my family, Donna and me. We especially thank You for that most wonderful

blessing of all, that blessing of bringing Donna and me together in true love.
And, then for giving us 22 years of wonderful, beautiful, glorious happiness
in true, unconditional love for each other and for You our Lord and Savior.
For these many, wonderful blessings, we thank you from the bottom of our hearts.
Lord, I know that You have resurrected Donna and brought her back to life in
Heaven. And I pray for You to bring us together again in Heaven in true
unconditional love for each other and for You our Lord and Savior, for eternity.
I pray for this, knowing that only You, our Lord and Savior can make it possible,
and with my obedient faith, believing in my heart that you will surely make it
come to pass. Lord, in the meantime I give myself to You, totally, to lead and
guide me in everything I do, everything I think, and everything I say, every minute
every hour of every day. Lead and guide me according to your will so that I may
become worthy of joining Donna in Heaven in truly unconditional love
for her and for You, when that is Your will for me. Thank you Lord for
helping me through every day of my life in everything I do. Amen.

Bill Belknap 2014

CONCLUSION

Writing "Unconditional Love and Faith Observed" has been the most rewarding experience of my life. The writing of this essay has brought about a much deeper understanding for me of my relationship with God and people, and a better understanding of what my whole life has been focused toward. Donna's unconditional love and Faith for God first and for me were a pivotal point in my life. She taught me through her deep devotion to these basic principals that until we accept and practice unconditional love and Faith in God, we have not become true Christian Believers. I understand now that through my deep love for Donna Kaye and her love for me, and both of our deep loves for our Lord God and Jesus Christ, I learned the true meaning of unconditional love and Faith. It took a lot of very serious thought, study and analysis for me to write this essay about observing both Donna's and my belief and trust in living our lives devoted to unconditional love and Faith. This effort of thinking and writing has brought the beauty and importance of unconditional love and Faith together for me to better understand the real underlying purpose and meaning of Christian life. That, in fact, once we give the reins of life over to God and let God do the driving, our life becomes very easy.

My mom and dad, my first wife, Carolyn, and our children, Barbara and Bill C. all provided me with unconditional love and Faith during my early life. When we are young we do not think much about these emotions and Beliefs, but in retrospect they were always there and were very important to our lives. My early family gave me the roots for a lifetime of unconditional love and Faith in God and in them. My essay relates a few of our family experiences of God taking good care of us and helping us to do what was best for us at all our times of need.

In looking back over my own personal life, my belief is that I practiced letting God lead my life for most all of my early life without even realizing that was what I was doing. My early Christian training and acceptance of God and Jesus Christ gave me the foundation to live a good Christian life, although my deep appreciation for the true meaning of unconditional love and Faith for God and for another person did not come to me until much later in my life.

My hope and prayer is that anyone reading my essay will understand and appreciate how wonderful and beautiful true unconditional love for and Faith in God and for another person can be and will always remember that God's truly unconditional love for each of us is perfection.

EPILOGUE

Since submitting the manuscript of this book to Westbow Publishers for them to begin work on publishing it, I have been involved in another wonderful experience of observing God's ever present help in our everyday lives. Often without prayer, God is there looking after us and providing us with our wants and needs without our asking. This latest experience started on April 1, 2015 which was April Fools Day. As the Wednesday morning Men's Prayer Group started their meeting that morning, Tari Carbaugh, our leader and Associate Pastor for Bartlesville First Church, phoned Dwayne Fifer from her pickup that our miniature donkey had gotten out and that she would be late because she was chasing the donkey down. We were all getting ready to go out and help her chase down the donkey when she drove up to McDonalds and announced "April Fool".

Being April Fool's Day, and since Tari and I had worked toward finding animals for our "petting zoo", which is becoming a coral, my thoughts were to fool her by asking her if she wanted a llama to join our other animals. At that time we had three horses, the miniature donkey and a baby lamb which was still on bottle. I was able to pull off my April Fool joke pretty well, Tari almost got "Oh that would be wonderful" out of her mouth when she looked into my face and said "April Fool". Of course we all had a good laugh.

My thoughts about acquiring a llama were not new that day, I had been thinking for some time that a llama would be a great addition to our coral. I knew there was a llama ranch near Grove, Oklahoma and was thinking seriously about driving over there to investigate buying a young llama, but had not gotten around to doing that yet.

Our baby lamb, Sam, which Tari is taking care of twenty four/seven needed to be cut (castrated) in order to become a good pet. So Tari took him to the Veterinary in Dewey, Oklahoma. While there, the assistant to the Veterinarian offered to give Tari, for Bartlesville First Church, a five month old male llama. What a surprise and what a wonderful gift. We now have our llama in the coral with our miniature donkey, Jethro. And, they are getting along well together and seem to like each other.

No one asked God for a llama or prayed for a llama that I know of, I believe God saw an opportunity and a need and matched them up for everyone's benefit. This experience certainly exemplifies for me how we can look around us in our everyday lives and see God at work everywhere. God is constantly doing things to help all of us with our daily lives by making things easier and better for us. My writing of this essay has opened my eyes to see and observe how much God is constantly doing for us without our asking. We need to thank Him in our regular prayers for all the wonderful things He does without our asking, as well as when we pray to Him asking for his blessings and help.

ABOUT THE AUTHOR

Bill Belknap was born on August 18, 1927 to William Albert Belknap and Earline Joe (Osborn) Belknap. His full name is William Bernhard Belknap, the Bernhard was his grandmother Belknap's maiden name. His father was an accountant and his mother a school teacher. As a child he was known as Billy B. From his birth date you can see he was a depression baby. His dad worked as an accountant for Cities Service Oil Company, and on the side, for supplemental income, operated a small dairy farm. His mother taught school before marriage, but was a home mother until Bill and his sister Mitzi were in Junior High School. Helping  on the dairy farm was an important influence on Bill's life. As everyone knows, who has worked or lived on a farm, farms are a good place to learn how to work, the facts of life, how to take care of live stock, milk cows and many other important lessons of life. This "basic training" in life was never forgotten by Bill and it has always been helpful to him.

Bill was a very good student throughout grade school and high school. He liked scouting and is an Eagle Scout. Other activities included music and sports. His good school record earned him a Henry L. Dougherty college scholarship from the oil company that employed his dad. He choose the engineering school at Oklahoma State University in Stillwater, Oklahoma. His college was paid for in thirds, one third by his scholarship, one third by his parents, and he worked and earned one third. Bill did exceptionally well in engineering school in college. Beginning with his sophomore year he taught mechanics and statics, and later strength of materials for his part of college costs. He was graduated with a B.S. degree in Civil Engineering and married Carolyn Crandell the last week of May 1949.

Immediately following marriage and college graduation, Bill went to work for Cities Service Oil Company as an engineering trainee. This trainee program gave him experience in the engineering functions of eight or nine departments of the company, but his permanent assignment became office work in oil and gas reservoir engineering. This work did not satisfy Bill because he wanted to learn how to drill oil wells and produce oil. His dissatisfaction lead to his changing jobs and companies after three years. He then went to work for Phillips Petroleum Company as a staff engineer in their district office in Ardmore, Oklahoma. About six months later, he was transferred to the North Texas District in Wichita Falls, Texas as district engineer. After three years in the field drilling oil wells and producing oil and two years in the company headquarters office, his career blossomed and during the mid sixties he worked in London as operations manager during the early drilling for oil and gas in the North Sea. From London, he returned to Bartlesville as chief engineer for Phillips International Operations. In the seventies, he was in Teheran, Iran working as regional manager for the middle east, and country manager for Iran. After the demise of Iran, he managed the Information Management Division for worldwide exploration and production operations. His last five years, before retirement in June 1986, were spent as Manager of Worldwide Drilling and Production Operations for Phillips Petroleum Company.

Following retirement from Phillips Petroleum, Bill did private petroleum and financial consulting. W.B. and Associates, Inc. was his company name. In addition to his consulting work, he spent considerable time as a volunteer in mission for the Good Shepherd Presbyterian Church where he was an Elder and Treasurer. He installed computer supported accounting systems and membership roll systems for that church. While doing this VIM work, he attended seminars on church administration at Union Seminary in Richmond, VA.

Bill's family life has experienced several major tragedies. Losing his daughter, Barbara, in 1973 from a bad automobile accident was devastating. In 1990 after fighting diabetes, then kidney failure, and finally a stroke, his wife of forty years, Carolyn, died taking a heavy tole on Bill. Finding Donna and marrying her in 1991 gave him and Donna some good years of enjoyable retirement until Bill had a stroke in May 2008. His left side was paralyzed, but with Donna's loving care, Faith in God, and good physical therapy he recovered except for some paralysis in his lower left leg and ankle and the need to walk with a cane. Donna had a devastating bleeding stroke two days before Christmas in 2012. She was hospitalized for six months before passing, and Bill stayed with her constantly during her hospitalization. Since Donna was twelve years younger than Bill this was a cataclysmic event for both of them. But, because of both of their strong and devout Faiths in God, Bill has persevered and became determined that he should document Donna's and his experience of finding unconditional love and faith for each other and for their mutual love and Faith in God. His determination following Donna's death resulted in his essay "Unconditional Love and Faith Observed".

Index to Photos and Copies